NOAH'S ARK ADVENTURES

5 Bedtime Stories of Courageous Creatures

BLUME POTTER

INTRODUCTION

Noah's Ark Adventures: 5 Bedtime Stories of Courageous Creatures is more than just a collection of stories—it's a treasure trove of timeless lessons wrapped in the warmth of bedtime storytelling. Each tale brings the beloved Bible story of Noah's Ark to life through the eyes of the animals, offering your children and grandchildren a fresh and engaging perspective on faith, courage, and friendship.

These stories are designed to not only entertain but also to inspire. As your little ones drift off to sleep, they will carry with them the comforting messages of trusting in God's plan, finding strength in unity, and the joy of new beginnings. The gentle, witty prose and endearing characters make this book a perfect addition to your family's nightly routine, fostering a love for the Bible and its teachings.

Give your children or grandchildren the gift of adventure, faith, and sweet dreams with Noah's Ark Adventures: 5 Bedtime Stories of Courageous Creatures—a must-have for every home that cherishes the beauty of God's promises.

CHAPTER ONE:
THE CALL TO THE ARK

In a quiet meadow, where the grass danced in the breeze and the flowers whispered secrets to the butterflies, a group of animals went about their usual day. The rabbits nibbled on clover, the squirrels darted up and down the trees, and the birds chirped their cheerful songs. Everything seemed as it always had been—until a strange feeling settled over the land.

From the distant horizon, a soft, echoing voice called out, "Come to the Ark. Come to the Ark." The animals paused, ears twitching and hearts pounding. What was this mysterious call? Why did it seem to speak directly to them?

In the center of the meadow, two small rabbits huddled close together, their noses twitching with anxiety. "Why would we need to go anywhere?" asked Thistle, the younger of the two. "We're just little rabbits. What could be so important that we must leave our home?"

Beside them, a pair of squirrels, Nutmeg and Chestnut, shared worried glances. "We're so small," Nutmeg squeaked. "What if we get lost or left behind? And what is this Ark, anyway?"

Just then, a large shadow fell over them. Looking up, they saw Noah—a kind man with gentle eyes, holding out his hands to them. His voice, warm and reassuring, spoke directly to their fears. "Do not be afraid, little ones. The Ark is a place of safety, built by God's command. He has chosen each of you for a special journey. Though you are small, you are important."

The rabbits and squirrels exchanged hesitant looks. "But why us?" Chestnut asked, his voice trembling. "We're just ordinary creatures."

Noah smiled. "God sees value in every creature, no matter how small. Sometimes, we don't understand His plans, but we must trust that He knows what is best. This is a journey of faith."

Though still uncertain, the animals felt a spark of courage in their hearts. If God had called them, then surely there was a reason, even if they didn't yet understand it. One by one, they nodded, deciding to follow Noah's lead.

As they made their way toward the Ark, they whispered words of encouragement to each other, their initial fears slowly melting away. The rabbits hopped alongside the squirrels, and together they embarked on the mysterious journey, trusting that the call to the Ark was part of a greater plan.

And so, the smallest creatures of the meadow took their first steps toward a grand adventure, learning that even when things didn't make sense, following God's call would always lead them to the right place.

CHAPTER TWO:
THE GREAT GATHERING

The path to the Ark was filled with the sounds of footsteps, hooves, and wings as animals from all corners of the earth heeded the mysterious call. From the tallest giraffes to the tiniest insects, every creature seemed to know that something extraordinary was happening.

Among the travelers were two very different pairs: a family of mighty elephants and a small group of timid mice. The elephants moved slowly and steadily, their massive feet thudding softly on the ground, while the mice scurried along, darting between blades of grass to avoid being stepped on.

At first, the elephants barely noticed the tiny mice below them. After all, what could such small creatures possibly have in common with giants like themselves? But as the journey continued, the elephants encountered a steep hill. The ground was loose and slippery, making it difficult for the elephants to climb.

As the lead elephant, Matilda, tried to find her footing, her trunk reached out for something to hold onto, but there was nothing within reach. The other elephants stumbled and slipped, unable to find a way up.

Below, the mice watched in concern. Though they were small, they had quick minds and nimble bodies. "We can help!" squeaked Pip, the smallest of the mice.

The elephants paused, looking down at the tiny creatures. "How could you help us?" Matilda asked, her deep voice filled with doubt.

"We may be small, but we know how to find the best paths," Pip replied confidently. "Follow us, and we'll lead you to the top!"

The elephants exchanged glances, unsure if they should trust the tiny mice. But with no other options in sight, they decided to give it a try.

The mice led the way, finding narrow paths and firm ground that the elephants could use to climb the hill.

Slowly but surely, the elephants followed, each step becoming easier as they trusted the mice to guide them.

When they reached the top, the elephants let out a triumphant trumpet, grateful for the unexpected help. "Thank you, little friends," Matilda said, lowering her trunk in a gesture of appreciation. "We wouldn't have made it without you."

The mice smiled proudly, feeling a warmth in their hearts. "We're all on this journey together," Pip replied. "It's not about how big or small we are; it's about helping each other along the way."

As they continued toward the Ark, the elephants and mice walked side by side, no longer seeing each other as different but as friends who had come together for a common purpose. Along the way, they shared stories and laughed, realizing that their differences made them stronger when they worked together.

And so, with new friendships formed and a spirit of unity guiding them, the animals continued their journey to the Ark, knowing that cooperation would see them through whatever challenges lay ahead.

CHAPTER THREE:
THE STORM BEGINS

As the animals settled into the Ark, a strange stillness filled the air. The sky, once clear and blue, now grew dark with heavy clouds, and a strong wind began to howl around them. The birds, usually so free and full of song, huddled together in their nests, their feathers ruffled with unease.

Outside, the first drops of rain began to fall, gently at first, but soon turning into a downpour. The sound of raindrops hitting the Ark echoed like the beating of a thousand drums. The floodwaters started to rise, covering the ground and creeping up the sides of the Ark.

Inside, the animals watched with wide eyes as the world they knew disappeared beneath the water. The lions roared softly in concern, the rabbits trembled in their burrows, and even the mighty elephants stood quietly, unsure of what was to come.

Among the most troubled were the birds. Accustomed to flying high above the trees, they now found themselves confined to the Ark. "What will happen to us?" a young sparrow named Skye chirped nervously. "We can't fly in this storm, and the world outside is disappearing!"

Nearby, an old owl named Orion spoke gently to the frightened birds. "We must trust in God's plan, little ones. This Ark was built to keep us safe. Though we cannot soar through the skies right now, we are sheltered here for a reason."

"But it's so hard to be stuck inside," Skye replied, her wings twitching with anxiety. "We don't know how long this storm will last."

Orion nodded wisely. "True, it is difficult to face the unknown. But remember, God brought us here and He will see us through this storm. Our wings may be grounded for now, but our hearts can still soar with faith."

The birds listened to Orion's words, finding comfort in his calm voice. They nestled closer together, choosing to believe that they were safe under God's protection.

As the storm raged on outside, the Ark became a refuge for all the creatures. Though fear and uncertainty tried to creep into their hearts, the animals leaned on each other and remembered Noah's words about trusting in God's plan.

The rain continued to pour, and the Ark swayed gently on the rising waters, but inside, the animals began to feel a sense of peace. They were not alone in this journey; they had each other, and more importantly, they had faith that they were exactly where they needed to be.

And so, amidst the storm, the animals held on to hope, knowing that the Ark would keep them safe until the waters receded and the world outside was ready for them once again.

CHAPTER FOUR:
LIFE ABOARD THE ARK

As the days turned into weeks, the animals on the Ark began to adjust to their new life. The storm still raged outside, but inside, they found ways to make the best of their unusual situation. Living together in close quarters was not always easy, especially for those who were natural enemies.

In one corner of the Ark, the lions rested quietly, their powerful bodies stretched out as they watched the other animals. Nearby, a small group of lambs huddled together, their soft bleats filled with worry. The lambs knew that outside the Ark, they would be considered prey, and they couldn't help but feel nervous being so close to the lions.

One day, as the lions yawned and stretched, one of the lambs, a young one named Lila, accidentally wandered too close. She froze, her heart pounding in her chest. The lioness, Nala, noticed Lila and slowly approached her, her eyes soft and calm.

Instead of pouncing or growling, Nala bent down and gently nudged Lila back toward the other lambs. "Don't be afraid," Nala said in a soothing voice. "We are all here to survive this storm together. There is no need for fear among us."

Lila blinked in surprise. "But aren't you supposed to hunt us? We've always been afraid of you."

Nala smiled, a gentle expression that seemed out of place on such a fierce creature. "Outside the Ark, yes, that is how things were. But here, we must learn to live in harmony. We are all under God's protection, and He has given us this time to be at peace with one another."

The lambs slowly began to relax, realizing that the lions meant them no harm. Over the next few days, the predators and prey learned to share the same space, understanding that their survival depended on cooperation and patience. The lions no longer saw the lambs as food, and the lambs no longer trembled in fear.

Instead, they found small ways to help each other. The lions, with their strength, helped to move heavy objects, while the lambs offered warmth and comfort to those who needed it. The Ark, though crowded, became a place of unexpected friendships and understanding.

As the days passed, the animals discovered that living in harmony required patience and kindness. They learned to overlook their differences and focus on the common goal of getting through the storm together.

And so, life aboard the Ark became a lesson in peace and cooperation. The animals realized that, despite their natural instincts, they could live together in harmony when they chose to see each other not as enemies, but as companions on a shared journey. The Ark was more than just a refuge from the storm—it was a place where God's creatures learned the true meaning of unity.

CHAPTER FIVE:
THE FIRST RAINBOW

After many days and nights, the rain finally stopped, and the Ark gently came to rest on solid ground. Inside, the animals could feel the change—they knew that something special was about to happen. The air was filled with a sense of anticipation and excitement.

Noah opened the Ark's door, and sunlight streamed in, brighter and warmer than they had remembered. One by one, the animals began to step outside, their eyes wide with wonder. The world looked different now—fresh and new, with the scent of wet earth and blooming flowers filling the air.

The young animals were the first to dash out, their hearts leaping with joy. The rabbits hopped around in the soft grass, the birds spread their wings and soared into the sky, and the lion cubs playfully pounced on each other, no longer bound by the confines of the Ark.

Lila, the little lamb, was among the first to explore the new land. She raced across the open field, her legs feeling strong and free. Nearby, Skye the sparrow flew higher than she ever had before, her tiny wings carrying her up toward the clouds. Everywhere, the animals reveled in their freedom, their fears and worries washed away by the joy of the moment.

As they explored, a hush suddenly fell over the crowd. The animals looked up to see something extraordinary—a brilliant arc of colors stretching across the sky. It was the first rainbow, a sight unlike anything they had ever seen.

Noah gathered the animals around and spoke in a voice full of reverence. "This rainbow is a sign of God's promise. He has brought us through the storm, and now He gives us this new world to live in peace and harmony. The rainbow is His covenant, a promise that He will never flood the earth again."

The animals gazed at the rainbow in awe, its colors vibrant and full of life. It was a symbol of hope and a reminder of the journey they had taken together. The lions and lambs stood side by side, the birds perched on the branches of newly sprouted trees, and the elephants trumpeted softly in contentment.

As the rainbow shimmered above them, the animals felt a deep sense of gratitude. They had survived the great flood, learned to live together in peace, and now they were ready to begin a new chapter in this fresh, beautiful world.

With the rainbow as their guide, the animals knew that they could face whatever the future held. They had each other, they had faith, and they had the promise of God's protection. And so, with hearts full of hope and joy, they began their new life under the colors of the first rainbow, a symbol of a brighter tomorrow.

www.ingramcontent.com/pod-product-compliance
Lightning Source LLC
Chambersburg PA
CBHW082041150726
47996CB00016B/3253